Will Writing For The Single Daddy

How To Write A Will For The Single Dad

Nick Thomas

Copyright © 2015 Nick Thomas

Visit my website at www.singledaddydating.com

ISBN-13: 978-1505405705

ISBN-10: 150540570X

JOIN OUR COMMUNITY!

Single Daddy Dating is a growing community of single fathers who look to help each other, not only with dating success but in all areas of their lives too. This includes parenting, career and finances advice.

Join us today and get '**10 Crucial Checklist To Dating Success For Single Fathers**' completely FREE!

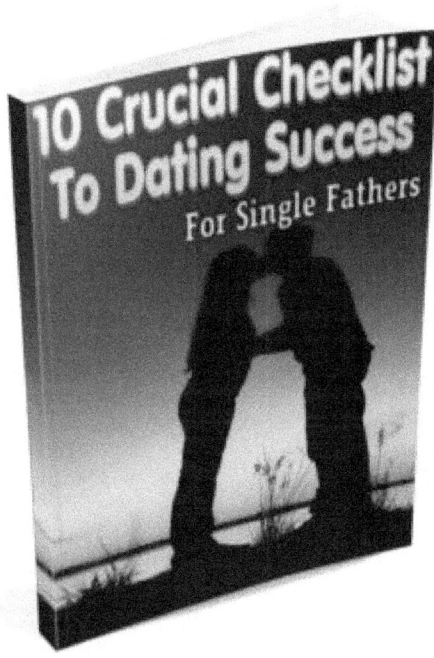

NICK THOMAS

CONTENTS

Chapter 1: What Is A Will

One of the most important tools for estate planning is the Will. A Will is a declaration made by a testator, the person who is making the Will that states what he/she wants to take effect after he or she is dead.

It is the last wishes of a person once they have passed on. In creating a Will, it would help pave the way for a person's assets to be distributed according to his wishes and instructions to others.

In making a will, a Will would commonly have these general characteristics. I wouldn't be able to speak for all countries, but I haven't heard of any laws in a country that doesn't follow these characteristics.

Among the general characteristics of a Will include:-

(1)   Wills Are A Declaration Of Intention

Writing a will doesn't mean that it is a contractual agreement. For example, if you decide to pass over your property to your son when you pass away, it doesn't mean that you pass it on immediately. It is merely a declaration of intention of what you intend to do after you have passed on.

During your lifetime, you can still dispose your property. A will wouldn't affect your power to dispose your assets if you have a need for it. Your son wouldn't be 'receiving' the property under the will, although there hasn't been a format revocation of the will.

(2)   Wills Are More Than For Property Disposal Purposes

Most people think that the purpose of a Will is to simply transfer your assets after you have passed on.

However, it is more than it. Will can also be used to revoke all the earlier Wills created, appoint guardian for the children who are minors or appoint specific individuals to perform specific tasks.

After a person passes on, he or she may have specific tasks that is part of his/her wishes. It may be continuing a business and appointing trustees.

You can also add in directives about your burial or cremation desires and if you wish to use your organs for medical transplants. There are some people who also wish to send loving notes to their family members through the use of a Will.

(3)   Wills Must Be In The Prescribed Form

For a Will to be in effect, it has to be followed the prescribed form set by the law. It should always be in writing, whether handwritten, typed or printed; and in any language.

For it to be in effect, the testator would need to sign or affix his signature at the end of the Will. It should be obvious that it has the intention of making the Will effective.

Besides that, a minimum of two people would also need to witness the signature of the Will by the testator or the person signing it on his behalf. These two witnesses would also need to attest to prove that the testator is signing it on his own behalf.

(4)   Wills Take Effect Upon Death

Until the testator is death, the beneficiaries and executors would have no power/rights over the estates. Therefore, a Will is capable

of dealing with other acquired assets after the Will is written.

If you have acquired other property or shares after the Will is written, you can still distribute it upon your death. The Will would need to be written in such a way that takes into effect possible acquisition of future assets.

(5) A Will Is Revocable

Before the testator's death, a will could be revoked. This could be done voluntarily of because of certain events that has happened in his lifetime. These are the few situations where the Will can be revoked:-

- **A New Will Is Written.** Whenever a new Will is written, the previous Wills are all revoked. We would want to change the contents of our Wills from time to time to reflect the changes in circumstances or our personal beliefs.

- **Marriage.** If a person is single during the

time of Will writing, a marriage would automatically revoke the previous Wills. If a single guy has intention to get married in the future, he can state his Will in such a way that takes into account the future marriage. However, the name of the future spouse should be clearly stated in the Will. If worded correctly, the Will would remain valid even after marriage.

- **Will Is Destructed.** Should the will get destroyed with an intention to revoke, it would be considered revoked. However, it doesn't mean that the Will is revoked should there be an accidental destruction or destruction by a third party. The court would still accept a copy of the original if it can be proven that the original has been destroyed without approval from the testator.

- **Execution In Writing.** The testator could state clearly in writing that he has intention to revoke a certain Will that is written in the past. Again, he would need to sign this document in the presence of two witnesses. The witnesses would need to attest to his signature.

A Will is one of the most important thing you can do to help your children if you pass on unexpectedly. It is especially important for a single father...

Chapter 2: A Will Is A Must Have

Everyone should have a Will. For a single father, it is a MUST HAVE.

Why is that so?

Your children depend on you now for their well-being. They need to be protected and be secured. Imagine if something unexpected happen to you. How would they continue their lives?

Even if you have many assets, it can be hard to be transferred to your children for them to benefit. Even if it is possible to transfer those assets to them, it would be difficult for them to manage those assets if they are too young. Therein lies the great importance of a Will.

If you are in a common two-parent family, it is still possible for your wife to take care of your children. If you are divorced and you don't feel comfortable leaving your assets to your ex-wife, you need to think about what to do.

These are the various reasons why a single father need a Will.

• **Minimise Hassle**

Very few people understand the pain of losing someone. The emotional rollercoaster can be difficult, but the aggravation from intestacy (dying without having a will) can compound the pain. If you die without a Will, it would be a big hassle for those who are still living. There are many cases where it takes years for the assets to be transferred to the living. If you have a Will, the transfer probably takes less than a year. It would minimize the hassle and ensure that the assets are distributed properly.

• Protect Your Assets And Loved Ones

Having a properly written Will helps you decide who would benefit from your estate and the portion you want them to receive. Without having a Will, your estate would be distributed based on the legal provisions. People who are dependent on your assets may not receive anything. A Will helps protect them, by transferring those assets to them.

• Exercise Of Right

A Will is in fact a legal right that you have. If you let go of this right, your living ones would be the one who suffer. It is a right where you allow your living loved ones to have right over the assets that you have. It also allows you the right to appoint a guardian for your minor children.

• Letters Of Administration Would Be Needed

After your death and if you die intestacy (without a Will), letters of administration would be needed for your estate to be distributed. This is needed because an administrator would need to be appointed to manage and distribute your estate according to the law.

Before someone can become an administrator, he/she would need to obtain consent from all beneficiaries before being allowed to act. This can take some time because it would be difficult to choose one that is all beneficiaries agree upon.

• People Who Are Unrecognised By Law Isn't Protected

There are certain people whom the law doesn't recognize. This includes unmarried partners, stepchildren and aged relatives. Since they aren't recognized by the law, if you die without a Will, their interests would not be protected as there aren't special provision to cater to their needs.

***

As you get a better insight as to what a Will is and its importance, many single fathers would ask if they should write a will. Even when I have shared the various benefits, many people can still be skeptical.

Many people argue that they don't have a lot of assets and would only write a will when they have more money. This is a wrong perception.

If you aren't blessed with many assets, it can be even more important to write a Will. If you aren't rich and have dependents, writing a Will can be even more important as your dependents would depend on your assets.

You would want it to be transferred as soon as possible.

If you were to really look at what you own, you would find that you do indeed own something. Everyone own at least a few things such as savings, fixed deposits or even a car. As such, it is important to remember that having a Will is very important. Especially for a single father.

Chapter 3: Types Of Wills

Before you start to get a Will written, you need to realize that there are various types of Wills. Every Will has a different purpose and you would need to be clear about their purpose before you start to make yours.

1. **Individual Wills.** This is the most common type of Will. Every individual would have different needs and it would need to be expressed in a different manner. This has to be written individually.

2. **Joint Wills.** This kind of Wills are made

when there are two or more people who wish to state their final wishes in a single document. Their desires would be executed according to the legal formalities. A joint Will wouldn't take effect like an individual Will. This is considered separate for each party involved. It is generally not recommended to have joint Wills as there would be certain issues of confidentiality if someone in the Will dies first. The Will would be read out and the other living person's wishes would be let known.

3. **Mutual Wills.** Mutual Wills are made by two or more people who have a mutual agreement between them to make such a Will. Besides that, an agreement would also be undertaken to not revoke the Will unless every party in the Will consent to it. In mutual Wills, there would normally be a sharing of the benefits.

4. **Living Wills.** A living Will is a written statement made by a person to inform

doctors who are treating him for a terminal medical situation. He may decide to discontinue treatment in certain situations if it means that he would only be artificially prolonging his life.

These four wills should be understood as there are various importance to each. As a single father, the two types of Will that would impact you the most would be <u>Individual Wills and Living Wills</u>.

You want to ensure that your children are protected. Individual Wills help easily transfer your assets and fulfil your final wishes for them. The importance of Living Wills meanwhile is relative. I have known some people who wouldn't want to get medical treatment if the costs of it seems too high. This all depends on the individual.

Chapter 4: General Contents Of A Will

To ensure that a Will is effective, there are some clauses that should be apparent. These are important to ensure a Will is acceptable to the legal jurisdiction. The various clauses include:-

1. **Opening Clause.** Every will would have an opening clauses with the testator's information. Should you have another name or an alias other than your given name, you need to state it clearly. Besides that, the date in which the Will is made is also important.

2. **Revocation Clause.** A revocation clause is placed after the opening clause where it is stated clearly that other earlier Wills would be revoked.

3. **Appointment Of Executor.** An executor is someone responsible to administer the deceased's estate upon death. You can appoint up to four executor, but it is always appropriate to appoint more than one executor. This is to ensure that there is a substitute 'executor' if one passes away. In the writing of a Will, the choice of executor is perhaps the most important part. He/She would be in charge of your estate and your last wishes. They would act on your behalf. Before appointing an executor, you would need to ask them for their permission first.

4. **Appointment Of Trustee.** Should you have children who are too young and can't be trusted with the responsibility of handling too much money, a trustee can be

appointed. This trustee would have the power over the money. However, you can also limit the scope of power they have over this sum of money. There are also other powers that can be transferred to others such as the power to run their business or invest in certain projects.

5. **Appointment Of Guardians.** Guardians are people who are responsible for the protection of your children if you were to die suddenly. If you are still married and you die unexpectedly, your wife would automatically be the guardian. However, if both of you suddenly die, this becomes very important. Like the appointment of an executor, you would also need to ask the permission of someone before appointing them as a guardian.

6. **Asset Distribution.** In the Will, you should have a guideline on how you want your assets to be distributed and in what proportions. To ensure that it is

distributed properly, seek for advice from someone who is experienced. Ask someone with the right professional expertise. The best person is a professional Will Writer. You can even get a Will writing software that can assist you with the process. Check it out at:-

www.singledaddydating.com/willwriter

7. **Residuary Clause.** This clause is included to dispose any assets that isn't specifically disposed in the Will. If such a clause isn't included, your assets would be distributed based on intestacy laws. Your wishes wouldn't be realised completely.

8. **Specific Instructions.** Everyone has their own specific instructions. This may be how you want things to be after you have passed away. This may be burying or cremating your body, or other funeral arrangements. You can also include some personal messages to your loved ones.

These are normally known as 'Terms Of Endearment'.

9. **Testamentary Trust.** There are times where you want your assets to be distributed over a certain period of time. This is because the beneficiaries aren't mature or old enough to handle such large amount of money. Setting up a testamentary trust helps because the distribution can be staggered in the combination that you desire. This eliminates the fear that money would be squandered.

These are nine main aspects that all Wills have. There are various purposes of each elements. As you understand better those different elements, you need to think about the various desires that you want when you pass on.

Even if you have written a Will, remember that you can still change it. You may acquire more assets or have more money in the bank. Your beneficiaries may also die, and this would impact your distribution of the assets.

Major changes such as a divorce or marriage would also impact the Will. Therefore, you need to look to update your Will from time to time whenever there are major changes in your life.

Chapter 5: Basics Of Will Writing

It is always better to get professional services when it comes to Will writing. A professional would be able to address all areas and avoid ambiguity when your Will is being read to the beneficiaries.

Having the Will written well would ensure that your desires are being communicated as you wouldn't be able to do so since you're already dead.

Before a Will is written properly, there would be certain formalities that would need to be followed before it could be considered valid in the court of law. Your professional Will writer would be able to ensure that they are fulfilled. Among the formalities include:-

- **Statement That The Testator Is Of Sound Mind.** When making the Will, the testator should be of sound mind. The testator should be clear about what he or she is doing, that is being of 'sound mind'. If the testator is writing the Will while he or she is on his dead bed, a professional doctor should be one of the witness to ensure he or she is of sound mind. If the Will is being contested, then the doctor would be called to court to give his evidence.

- **Testator's Age.** The minimum age of the testator would be different in each country. However, for most countries, the minimum age is 18.

- **Will In Writing.** The Will would need to be in writing, either typed or handwritten.

An oral Will wouldn't be sufficient unless it is a privileged Will. Privileged Wills are wills made orally by soldiers, airman or mariners at seas. They are usually employed in an expedition or engaged in warfare.

- **Signature Or Affixation.** This would be required to confirm that the Will is valid. If the testator is incapable of doing so, someone could sign on his behalf.

- **Attestation.** To ensure that the Will is valid, it needs to be attested by two witness who are present during the signature. Their signature would also be needed in the Will.

The process of drawing up a Will is very simple once you understand the various issues involved. The following questions should be considered when writing a Will:-

- **Are You Looking For A Professional**

Will Writer? From a legal perspective, everyone could write a Will. However, a professional Will writer would be better as they have more experience and know what to expect. Even if they cost money, it would be more worth it over the long term. Having a professional Will writer write your Will would ensure that your Will wouldn't be contested in court.

- **Who Is Your Executor?** Do you have someone you trust and can rely upon as an executor? This is the most important issue to consider in preparing a Will. The executor would have the responsibility to execute your Will and your other affairs when you are gone. Make sure to ask him/her for permission before you appoint him/her.

- **Who Would Be Guardians?** Do you need to get a guardian for your children who are minors? Who is good with children and able to be a good role model for your children? If this is a factor, then you would need to have a deep thought about this. Similar to finding an executor, you also need to ask for consent from the guardian.

- **Who Are Your Beneficiaries?** Think about who you want to benefit from your estate. Normally, this would be your children and spouse. As a single father, your main beneficiaries would be your children. However, you wouldn't want them to have all your estate immediately. You need to have a deep thought about anyone whom you want to benefit from your estate and this may include the person you want to take care of your children.

These four questions are the main issues that you would need to consider before drawing up your Will. It is important to give these questions deep thought before you even start to find a professional Will writer.

If you have thought these questions through, it would be easier for you to gain the most from Will writing. You would have thought about the various possibilities after you are gone.

Chapter 6: Keep The Will Safe

After your Will has been drawn up, you need to consider how to keep your Will safe. Keeping your Will safe is as important as the privacy of the information inside the will. You would want the information in the Will to be private and confidential.

Wills need to be kept safely to preserve the confidentially as you wouldn't want other people to see your Will and try to tamper with it. If you keep it yourself, you need to let certain trustable people know. This may be your executors. If you are dead, they would know where to locate your Will.

Generally, most testators would decide to keep the Will in a safe deposit box in the bank or other secret location. During such situations, it can be difficult because in the event of a death of the testator, the safe deposit box would be frozen and the Will wouldn't be able to be taken out.

If you keep it elsewhere and no one knows about it when you die, it also creates the same problem. You might as well not write it in the first place.

To prevent any loss from happening, the Will should be kept by someone whom you trust. In such a situation, you must choose someone whom you trust completely. The person keeping it must keep it securely too.

Even if this arrangement seems feasible, there isn't any guarantee that the Will can be located. The person you have entrusted to keep the Will may misplace or even predeceased you. In such a case, the purpose of writing a Will would be lost too.

A better way of keeping the Will safe would be to use professional will custody service. It would prevent tampering and destruction. It has a safer way of keeping and easier retrieval. Many companies are offering such services nowadays and they have many benefits. Among them include:-

- **Protection From Destruction.** These companies spend a lot of money in protecting those Wills. You would feel better knowing your Will is safe from potential destructions such as a fire, flood or burglary.

- **No Tampering.** When your Will is kept safe, tampering cannot be done. No one would have access to your Will.

- **Controlled Access And Confidential.**

These services would have a system of personal identification cards and a safe retrieval process. This prevents your Will from being exposed to other people. Only you would have access to your Will during your lifetime and your executors upon death.

- **Personalised Service.** These service would contact you annually and offer other forms of service that may help you. They would update you on the law regarding Wills or other financial services that may help you. These services may also include financial planning services to ensure that you can locate your assets easily. If you plan your assets properly, your executors wouldn't need to hunt your assets before administrating them.

- **Provide Free Insurance.** Many people don't know this, but certain professional will custody service offer free insurance as well. Certain corporation provide free personal accident insurance to testators who keep their Wills with them.

It is clear that professional will custody service is the way to go. Keeping your Will on your own or with other people can be way too dangerous. There could be future problems that you can't anticipate. Most people who write their wills would store them in such professional will custody service.

In fact, most professional Will writers would already combine a package together with will custody services. Spend some time looking for one that has a great deal that combines both writing and custody of the Will.

Chapter 7: Personal Representatives

In many parts of this book, I have mentioned about the importance of the 'personal representatives'. This includes the executor and administrator of the deceased estate. There are various other representatives that would play a big part in ensuring that the testator's last wishes are met.

In this chapter, you would learn in more detailed about the various representatives together with its importance.

Executor

An executor is a person or corporate body (Trust Corporation) who specializes in the management of the affairs of the estate or other important trust matters.

The rights and duties that is being conferred to a trust corporation is similar to that of an individual personal representative. They would need to abide by the legal requirements and other orders set by the court.

From previous chapters, I have said that when appointing an executor, the testator can appoint an individual or a few more. This is up to four. If a beneficiary is a minor, it is ideal to have a minimum of two executors. This is unless a trust corporation is appointed to administer the estate.

Administrator

The person or trust corporation being appointed by the court in the case of intestacy (no Will made by deceased) would be called the administrator. An administrator might even be used should the deceased wrote a Will but didn't name an able executor or where the executor predeceased him.

Trustee

Generally, the function of a personal representative is to wind up the estate and distribute the assets. The function of a trustee meanwhile, is to hold up the assets until an event has happened. It may be a beneficiary reaching the age of majority.

In most situations, the testator would appoint the same person to be the trustee and executor. Depending on the law of the state, the trust may be created expressly by the Will but in other situations, it arises because of the operation of the law. The operation of the law occurs when there are minor beneficiaries and those gifts aren't able to be distributed to them.

Choosing An Executor

It should be clear by now that the executor is the most important role in a Will. When it comes to administrating a deceased's estate, an executor would help in ensuring that the wishes are being met.

An executor needs to have many qualities and many people are often finding it hard to choose one. Even if they find one, they aren't sure if the other person is willing. The following are issues that you need to consider in the selection of an executor:-

• **Age**

This is a major consideration because it you get someone who is too old and the executor dies before the testator, it would create a problem. The administration of the estate would need to be done by letters of administration and can become tricky. However, if you get someone who is too young, he or she may not have the maturity to execute the Will if it doesn't has detailed instructions.

• **Willingness And Capacity To Act**

This is the most important factor. You want the executor to be willing to act upon the testator's death. He should also be capable of doing it. If there aren't any executor at the time of the testator's death, it is more or less the same as not naming any executor in the first place.

Make sure that you gain the consent of

the executor(s) before you appoint him or her. For many people, they choose to appoint their spouses as an executor. It seems convenient, but it can sometimes be a bad idea because a grieving spouse wouldn't be in the right state of mind to execute your Will.

• **Integrity**

A person's estate would be what they work for their entire lives. When appointing an executor, the testator is entrusting the executor with great responsibility because he is 'giving' him rights over his entire estate.

It is hard to determine the integrity of a person unless you have known him well. He would need to trust the other person to act on his behalf. If you find it hard to find a suitable family members (due to incapability) or a trustworthy friend, it would be better to appoint a trust corporation.

• **Asset Management Skills**

Being an executor requires some skill. There isn't any specific training for this, but some people are better than others with managing assets. This is especially important if the testators has a lot of assets.

There are certain situations where the role of an executor is to continue the business or invest. Therefore, having some financial and business knowledge would help a lot.

Besides that, the executors would also need to have time to execute your Will. It would take a lot of time to administer your asset and it would only get worse if they have no idea how to do so.

***

In most situations, it can be tough to find an appropriate executor. Due to this, a trust corporation could be authorized to be the executor, trustee and investment manager.

These corporation have the skills needed and their experience would be invaluable. Besides that, they are known to be more professional and would understand the estate laws better. This means that your estate would be administered more efficiently and the last wishes can be fulfilled.

Chapter 8: Checklist To Will Preparation

The contents of this book is a simplified version of preparing a Will. It doesn't cover a lot of important areas as it is meant to simply give you a bare introduction to the importance of having a Will and the various areas you need to consider.

If you want to get more information about Will writing, it would be best if you get a professional Will writer to advice you.

From this book, I hope you are clear why

writing a Will is important, especially as a single father. This is a simple checklist before you start off with your Will writing. Among the areas include:-

- **Executors.** Who are your executors? Write down their names and determine if they are the right person to help you. See if they are trustworthy and responsible. You would need to ask their permission after this. Make sure they are willing.

- **Guardian.** Find a person who is responsible and good with children. He or she would be the guardian for your minor children, if you have them. Seek their permission. Then, get their personal details and address. This is similar to finding an executor.

- **Beneficiaries.** Who do you want as your beneficiary? List down all your beneficiaries and write down their details.

- **Assets.** List down all the assets that you have. Special notice should be given to the valuable assets such as land, property and cars. Other assets such as fixed deposit, jewellery and savings should also be written down.

- **Who Receives What?** Write down what asset would each beneficiary receives. This division should be such that there won't be any quarrels in the future between the beneficiaries.

- **Terms Of Endearment.** What special messages would you have for your loved ones?

- **Special Instructions.** How would you want your funeral to be conducted? How do you want to invest your money? Do you want to donate to any charities?

Once you have considered all these details, you can now get your professional Will writer write for you one. It would save you a lot of time because you have considered the main factors.

Chapter 9: Will Writing Resources

From experience, there are some will writing resources online that can really speed up the will writing process. The information in this book has a purpose to give you a rough idea of what to expect but I don't expect you to know how to write a will merely from the contents of this book.

For that, you can use the following resources that has helped many other single fathers I know. They have shared with me their experience of using these resources and I have personally validated how good they are.

Different people would have different needs. Therefore, I recommend that you take time to check out all these services before deciding on one.

(1) 10 Minute Will [UK-Based]

Link:
www.singledaddydating.com/10minuteWill

This service was recommended by a single father in London. His name is Joey. This online will writing service is valid for English & Welsh Law.

When I tried out this service, I am amazed by how quickly I can create one. The service uses questionnaires to clarify what I want. Yes, you can get a Will done in TEN MINUTES. Amazing.

(2) GlossLegal [UK-Based]

Link:

www.singledaddydating.com/glosslegal

This is another high quality service for those based in the UK. It is slightly more expensive than 10 Minute Will, but the good thing is that those wills are checked by a qualified solicitor.

The price difference isn't much actually. Therefore, if you are in the UK, I recommend that you check both those services.

(3) Global Wills

Link:

www.singledaddydating.com/globalwills

This is a worldwide service that can be used by anyone. What amazes me about this service is how thorough they are. You can get ALL YOUR ESTATE PLANNING needs from this website alone.

Besides, there is also a FREE ESTATE PLANNING GUIDE. Get the free guide at the

It is totally FREE!

(4) Now Legal [USA Based]

Link:

www.singledaddydating.com/nowlegal

This service is focused for USA based residence. Like most of the above service recommended, it has the similar service such as Will writing.

Besides that, you would also have other personal legal affairs documentation. They have a very simple interface that helps men who aren't well-versed with computers. Definitely worth checking out!

(5) Nolo

Link:

www.singledaddydating.com/nolo

Nolo is a service which is more catered towards professionals in the estate planning field. They have quality resources for you to read and software you can use to produce your Will.

For most single fathers, you won't need such detailed information. However, if you really want to know more about these legal information, this website has ton of valuable resources. In fact, many lawyers I know are utilising these resources.

***

I hope these resources can help you. Do check it out to find one that best suits your needs.

LEAVE A REVIEW

I hope this book has helped you well. It isn't my intention at all to go deep into the topic. I am no expert in everything. However, I have the help of many other single fathers who have shared with me their invaluable experience.

If this book has helped you in any way, do leave me a review. This helps build our single father community.

If you feel that this book can be improved in any way, do mention it in the review. I would love to hear from you.

I wish you luck as a single father…

ABOUT NICK THOMAS

Nicholas Thomas has helped many single fathers cope with divorce in the past few years. By helping them gain more confidence and stability in their lives, he is able to guide them towards being a man that attracts other women easily.

He divorced back in 2008 and knows how difficult a divorce can be for a man. It was a terrible time for him when he got his divorce. He envisioned his children blaming him and not being able to spend time with him. It gave him a constant guilt trip.

Being a divorced man can be very difficult. Ever since his 'emotional recovery' from the divorce, he has helped many single fathers by advising and helping them gain confidence.

Should you want to share your story with him, you can do so at www.singledaddydating.com/shareastory/

ALSO BY NICK THOMAS

(1) Dating After Divorce For The Single Daddy

(2) Dating Ideas For The Single Daddy

(3) How To Be An Alpha Male

(4) First Date Conversations

(5) Online Dating

(6) How To Approach Women

(7) Mature Dating

(8) Single Parent Support

(9) Coping With Divorce

(10) Parenting After Divorce

Visit www.singledaddydating.com/bookstore/

Get Your Complimentary
FREE BOOK

Join our community today and get **<u>10 Crucial</u>**
<u>Checklist To Dating Success For Single Fathers</u>
FREE, delivered right to your email…

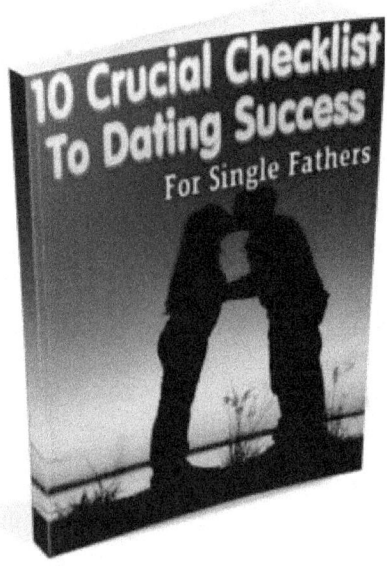

JOIN US AT
<u>WWW.SINGLEDADDYDATING.COM/</u>
<u>NEWSLETTER/</u>